# America's
# First Ladies

## 1865 to the present day

The White House in 1872

A Pull Ahead Book

# America's First Ladies

## 1865 to the present day

Lillie Chaffin
Miriam Butwin

Lerner Publications Company    •    Minneapolis, Minnesota

ACKNOWLEDGMENTS: The illustrations are reproduced through the courtesy of: pp. 5, 6, 9, 10, 12, 18, 19, 22, 24, 28, 29, 30, 32, 33, 34, 38, 39, 40, 41, 43, 46, 48, 55, 59, 61, 63, 65, 68, 70, 72, 74, 77, 78, 81, 82, 89, 94, 100, 104, Library of Congress; p. 15, Smithsonian Institution; pp. 16, 26, New York Public Library; p. 52, Theodore Roosevelt Association; p. 58, Culver Pictures, Inc.; p. 85, Independent Picture Service; p. 87, United States Army; pp. 91, 102, 106, Minnesota Democratic-Farmer-Labor Party; p. 96, National Republican Party; p. 109, Nixon-Agnew Campaign Committee, New York; p. 111, Nixon-Agnew Campaign Committee, Minneapolis; pp. 115, 117, National Archives; p. 120, Karl Schumacher, The White House; p. 123, Jack Kightlinger, The White House; pp. 126, 130, Michael Evans, The White House; p. 132, The White House.

Front cover photo: *Mrs. Eleanor Roosevelt* by Douglas Chandor, White House Collection

Back cover photo: Independent Picture Service

The Library of Congress cataloged the
original printing of this title as follows:

Chaffin, Lillie D.
    America's First Ladies. Minneapolis, Lerner Publications Co.
[1969]

    2 v. illus., ports. 21 cm. (A Pull Ahead Book)

    Brief biographies of thirty-eight First Ladies and White House hostesses from Martha Washington to Patricia Nixon.

    Contents—v. 1. 1789-1865.—v. 2. 1865 to present day.

    1. Presidents—U. S.—Wives—Juvenile literature. [1. Presidents—Wives] I. Butwin, Miriam, joint author. II. Title.

E176.2.C45                973 [920]                68-31499
ISBN 0-8225-0455-3 (v. 1); 0-8225-0456-1 (v. 2)

**1981 REVISED EDITION**

International Standard Book Number: 0-8225-0456-1
Library of Congress Catalog Card Number: 68-31499

6  7  8  9  10  90  89  88  87  86  85  84  83  82  81

Lou Hoover

# contents

Eliza Johnson lost a son and a son-in-law in the Civil War.
Both men served in the Union Army.

# Eliza McCardle Johnson
(1810-1876)

Eliza McCardle was born in Leesburg, Tennessee. Her father, a poor shoemaker, died when she was very young. At 16 she became a teacher in Greeneville, Tennessee. There she met Andrew Johnson, an 18-year-old tailor from North Carolina. He had never gone to school. He could read, but that was all. Eliza became his teacher. After their marriage in 1827 she taught him writing and arithmetic and helped him improve his spelling. They lived behind the tailor shop until they could afford to build a home.

Johnson was a good tailor and his business flourished. Soon craftsmen from all over town came to the shop to talk politics. They were joined by workers and farmers. All opposed the great landowners whom they felt had too much power in the state of Tennessee. Andrew Jackson was their hero.

In 1828, when Jackson became President, Andrew Johnson became an alderman on the town council of Greeneville. Then he was elected mayor. He served two terms in the Tennessee House and a term in the state senate. By 1843 he was ready for national politics. He entered the House of Representatives and began a 20-year battle to enact a homestead bill. His plan to provide western

land for poor farmers was opposed by Southern congress-
men who feared that new western territories would become
free states. The bill was not enacted until 1862 when
Johnson was the only Southerner left in the Senate. During
his 10 years in the House he steered a middle course on
the slavery issue. Johnson owned eight slaves. To him the
welfare of small farmers seemed more important than
the problems of large slaveowners, as later the Union
would matter more to him than the preservation of slavery.

In 1857, after two terms as governor of Tennessee,
Johnson was elected to the Senate. In the spring of 1861
he traveled by train throughout the state, urging the
people to vote against secession. Tennessee left the Union
but Johnson did not. An order went out for his arrest but
he escaped from the state before the militia could catch him.

In 1862 Union armies took Tennessee, and President
Lincoln appointed Johnson military governor of the state.
By 1864 he seemed a good choice for the vice-presidency.
He was a Democrat, but a loyal one, and his work in war-
time Tennessee fit well with Lincoln's plans for the post-
war South.

Johnson was Vice-President for six weeks. On April
14, 1865, he was called to Lincoln's bedside in the house
across the street from Ford's Theatre, where the President
had been shot. Early on the morning of the 15th Lincoln
died. Back in his hotel room Johnson was sworn in as
President.

Andrew Johnson
(1808-1875)

In Tennessee his family packed their belongings into two carriages and set off for Washington. They were a crowd: two grown sons, two married daughters (one widowed), five grandchildren, and Eliza. They arrived on a hot summer day and scattered about the house, picking out bedrooms and making plans for a clean-up. Eliza's health had been bad for many years. She chose a comfortable south bedroom, stocked it with books and yarn, and appointed her older daughter Martha hostess and housekeeper.

Martha Patterson, the Johnsons' eldest daughter, acted as White House hostess. Her husband was Senator D. T. Patterson of Tennessee.

Martha had the house scrubbed. New wallpaper and slipcovers made the reception rooms fresh and neat after years of rough use. Two Jersey cows roamed the White House lawn. Early every morning Martha, dressed in calico, came down to milk the cows before breakfast.

Eliza missed Tennessee and was not impressed with her position as First Lady. Even so, her personal strength and kindness were important throughout Johnson's presidency. She kept three families happy in one house, and gave quiet support to Johnson during his struggle with Congress.

Before the war, Johnson had not pleased the great Southern landowners, and now he failed to satisfy many Northern Republicans in Congress. They felt that his plans for Reconstruction of the South were too gentle — and that they would lose control of the South to native Democrats. The conflict between Johnson and Congress reached its peak early in 1868. In February the House voted to impeach him — to charge him with crimes against the state — and a few days later they decided upon a list of crimes. On March 13 his trial began. The Senate sat in judgment, presided over by Chief Justice Salmon P. Chase. Lawyers handled the case for Johnson, who did not come to the trial. In mid-May several of the charges were voted upon. By one vote Johnson was acquitted.

Late in 1868, after a new President had been elected, Johnson pardoned all Southerners who had taken part in the war, though Congress had planned to make this gesture. In March 1869 the Johnsons went back to Tennessee. Twice the ex-President ran for Congress and lost. In 1874 he was elected to the United States Senate. When he entered the chamber in March 1875, the Senators clapped, and several sent bunches of flowers to him. That summer in Tennessee Johnson had a stroke and died. A few months later Eliza died. She was buried next to him in Greeneville.

## Julia Dent Grant
(1826-1902)

Julia Dent was born in St. Louis, Missouri. Her prosperous father was a judge. She met Ulysses Simpson Grant when he was stationed in St. Louis with the Fourth Infantry Regiment. He had been a classmate of her brother at West Point. Julia and Grant became engaged. Then his regiment moved south. In 1846 he was in Texas when the Mexican War began. He fought in Mexico and after the war returned to St. Louis, where he and Julia were married on August 22, 1848.

For two years they lived at army posts in Michigan. When he was sent to another post, Julia returned to St. Louis where the first of their four children was born. Then Grant was ordered to go west, to Fort Vancouver in Oregon. He could not afford to support his family on army pay, so he did not take them along. Julia and her son Frederick went to live with Grant's parents in Ohio. In the West, Grant grew very lonely and unhappy and he began to drink. Finally he had to resign.

The Grants returned to St. Louis. They tried farming and business and failed in both. In 1860 they moved to Galena, Illinois, where Grant took a job in his brothers' leather store. He proved himself a poor shopkeeper.

In the spring of 1861 when the Civil War began, Grant volunteered. He wanted a federal commission but Washington did not answer his request. As a colonel of Illinois Volunteers he went to Missouri where he had a chance to practice some of the skills he had learned in Mexico. In August 1861 he was promoted to brigadier general. Grant won battle after battle in the Western campaign—Fort Donelson, Vicksburg, Chattanooga—and in March 1864 Lincoln made him commander of all Union armies. Grant came east and took charge of the last campaigns of the war, closing in upon Lee's forces at Richmond. Lee was routed from Richmond in April 1865, and he surrendered to Grant at Appomattox Court House a few days later.

Although Grant was criticized throughout the war for losing large numbers of men, his victories made him a national hero. He was soon drawn into politics, which had meant nothing to him before the war. For a time he supported Johnson's mild plan for the South, but by 1868 he had gone over to the radical Republicans who opposed Johnson. That summer the Republicans nominated him for President, and in November he defeated Democrat Horatio Seymour, an ex-governor of New York.

Julia considered the White House too small and uncomfortable for her tribe of children and relatives. She suggested that they live in their own Washington home and go over to the White House for the necessary parties and receptions. Grant vetoed the idea. The house was redecorated soon after they moved in, and in 1873 a major overhauling of the interior transformed it completely. The 1870's and 1880's are often called the Gilded Age. The new White House rooms were as elegant as the finest hotel lobby or Pullman dining car, and in keeping with the age, everything was trimmed with gold.

White House parties were equal to the decor. Grant himself was a rather shy man who avoided social life when he could and preferred the company of his family, his old friends, and his horses. But Washington after nearly a decade of wartime restraint was ready for a big splash.

Ulysses S. Grant (1822-1885) and his family, in 1868: (front) Jesse, Ulysses, Jr., and Julia; behind them, Nellie and Frederick with one of the Grant ponies.

Guests at state dinners were served 20- to 30-course meals. Women had a chance to display the most complicated outfits of the nineteenth century. They wore a series of under-skirts and over-skirts, often looping one skirt back to cover a bustle. Their gowns were trimmed with yards of fringe, ruffles, and lace.

Reporters filled the women's pages of the newspapers with costume details from the White House. They also wrote of the Grant family. Grandfather Grant and Grandfather Dent, two sharp old men, carried on a North-South rivalry, and always made good copy. But the press's favorite was Nellie Grant, the President's only daughter. A

Nellie Grant's wedding in the East Room, May 1874.
The wedding bell was made of flowers.

dropout after one day at boarding school, Nellie took a
trip to Europe with family friends. On the return voyage
she met a rich, handsome Englishman, Algernon Sartoris.
They were married in the White House in May 1874, just
before her 19th birthday. The East Room was packed with
flowers.

In 1872 Grant had been re-elected even though his administration was a hotbed of corruption. Grant trusted his friends and refused to believe that they could be dishonest. During his second term, congressional investigations revealed one scandal after another. In 1875 they discovered that Grant's private secretary, Orville Babcock, had protected the Whiskey Ring, a group of distillers who had withheld taxes from the government. Grant stood up for Babcock and got him off the hook.

By 1876 the Republican party needed a candidate free from any hint of scandal. They chose Rutherford B. Hayes of Ohio. Grant's friends in the party suggested that he take a long trip abroad in order to build up his popularity well before the 1880 convention. For two years the Grants traveled around the world and attracted great crowds everywhere. In 1880 Grant's men stuck with him for 35 ballots before yielding to a dark horse, James Garfield, on the 36th. Grant was relieved.

In 1881 the Grants moved from Galena to Mount McGregor in upstate New York. Grant tried his hand at one more business venture, investing his savings in a New York banking firm. The bank collapsed in 1884 and Grant lost all of his money. To support his family he began to write. He finished *Personal Memoirs* in 1885, two months before his death. The book was popular and provided well for Julia Grant in her later years. She died in 1902 and was buried with her husband in Grant's Tomb.

Lucy Hayes was the first President's wife to have a college degree. She was an active reformer and took part in the movement to abolish slavery.

# Lucy Webb Hayes

(1831-1889)

Lucy Webb was born in Chillicothe, Ohio. Her father was a doctor. Two years after her graduation from Wesleyan Female College in Cincinnati, she married Rutherford Birchard Hayes, a lawyer she had met at a summer resort.

Also an Ohioan, Hayes had graduated from Kenyon College and Harvard Law School. In Cincinnati he built up his law practice and was elected city solicitor in 1858.

Hayes, who loved to read, was a member of the Literary Club of Cincinnati. When the Civil War broke out, the Literary Club mustered up and got ready for battle. Hayes served with distinction, losing four horses which were shot from under him. In 1864 he was elected to the United States House of Representatives but he did not enter the House until the war was over. His committee assignment suited Hayes well—he was chairman of the Joint Committee on the Library of Congress.

Rutherford B. Hayes
(1822-1893)

By 1876 Hayes had served three terms as governor of Ohio. That summer the Republican convention was held in Cincinnati, his hometown. The party was split between supporters of Grant (who did not want a third term) and a group led by James G. Blaine, a congressman from Maine. The Grant die-hards were called *Stalwarts*. Their leader was Senator Roscoe Conkling of New York, who controlled the party in his state. Under Grant, Conkling had been able to give out all federal jobs in New York — a task which he did not want to lose. Blaine's men were the *Half-Breeds*. They tended to oppose the job-peddling of the Stalwarts, but the basis of their quarrel with the Stalwarts was a personal feud between Blaine and Conkling. At the Cincinnati convention neither side had enough votes to nominate. On the seventh ballot the delegates selected Hayes as a compromise candidate.

Hayes ran against the Democratic governor of New York, Samuel J. Tilden. The Democrats were on the upswing after years of defeat. Tilden got about 250,000 more popular votes than Hayes, but the electoral votes went to Hayes by a margin of one. A commission of eight Republicans and seven Democrats investigated the disputed votes of four states and gave them all to Hayes. Southern Democrats went along with the decision when they received a promise that Reconstruction would end. Hayes and his wife were on the way to Washington in March 1877 when the final word reached them.

On Inauguration Day, a Sunday, the Grants gave the last of their 20-course dinners for the new President and his wife. Six wine glasses stood at each plate, and garlands of flowers swung from the ceiling. A 10-foot pink azalea hovered behind Lucy Hayes's chair.

Later that spring, guests at White House dinners realized that the tables were bare of wine glasses. Rutherford and Lucy Hayes had long belonged to the temperance movement. At their first party one guest had become tipsy and they decided to drop liquor altogether. Soon the nickname "Lemonade Lucy" caught on. Lucy Hayes took the teasing with good humor.

Card-playing, smoking, and dancing were also forbidden at the White House. Lucy was a warm hostess at public receptions as well as at state affairs, but most of her parties seemed quiet after the Grants' and some people found them dull. The Hayes family most enjoyed meeting with a few friends in an upstairs sitting room, where they could play the piano and sing hymns.

Soon after he took office Hayes pulled the last federal troops out of South Carolina and Louisiana. Democratic politicians took over the South again and stopped complaining about Hayes's doubtful victory. His own party became disturbed when he pushed for civil service reform. Congress did nothing about it, but Hayes's actions angered the Stalwarts. In 1878 he dismissed Chester Alan Arthur

Secretary of the Interior Carl Schurz provides music for the Hayes family and their friends at a gathering in a White House parlor, 1880.

from his job in the New York Customs House without first consulting Roscoe Conkling. Fortunately, Hayes did not want a second term.

In March 1881, with his friend James Garfield in the White House, Hayes and his family went back to their home near Fremont, Ohio. He dropped politics entirely. He and Lucy resumed their old interest in prison reform, education, and the prohibition of alcohol.

# Lucretia Rudolph Garfield
(1832-1918)

Lucretia Rudolph was born near Garretsville, Ohio. Her father was a farmer. She met James Abram Garfield while they were both students at Hiram College. While he completed his studies at Williams College in Massachusetts, Lucretia taught in Cleveland.

In 1856 Garfield came back to Hiram to teach Latin and Greek. A year later, at the age of 26, he became president of the college. He began to study law and in his spare time he preached for the Disciples of Christ. He and Lucretia were married in 1858 and settled down on the college campus.

Garfield finished his law studies, was admitted to the bar, and entered the state legislature. In 1861 he volunteered for service in the Civil War, winning the rank of major general and the nickname of "Praying Colonel." Lucretia managed the home they had bought. In December 1863 Garfield went to Washington as a member of the House of Representatives, and for the next 17 years Lucretia divided her time between Washington and her Ohio home.

Two of the Garfields' seven children died in infancy, leaving them with four sons and a daughter, Mollie.

Lucretia Garfield

Lucretia's calmness and strength were important to
Garfield. Both of them liked books and encouraged their
children to read and to think.

During the 1870's Garfield, a Republican, found himself between the Stalwarts and the Half-Breeds and on fair
terms with both. At the time of the 1880 Republican con-

vention Garfield was a Senator-elect and head of the Ohio delegation. Again the Stalwarts and Half-Breeds fought, and neither Grant nor Blaine could get enough votes. Blaine's men threw their support to Garfield who was nominated on the 36th ballot. As a favor to the Stalwarts, Chester Alan Arthur of New York was given the vice-presidential nomination. His friend Roscoe Conkling assumed that the gift of the New York jobs would still be in his hands.

Garfield defeated General Winfield Scott Hancock, a veteran of the battle of Gettysburg, and returned to the war in his own party. He appointed James Blaine Secretary of State, and Conkling began to seethe. In other assignments, Garfield seemed to be overlooking the Stalwarts entirely. The offended Conkling resigned from the Senate. He expected the state legislature to re-elect him, but it did not.

Job-seekers continued to line the stairs at the White House. Garfield had never been a reformer, but he began to feel that some changes in the civil service system would be a good idea.

In early May, two months after Garfield's inauguration, Lucretia came down with malaria. When she recovered the family went to Elberon, New Jersey, to rest by the sea. Back in Washington Garfield prepared to go to a class reunion at Williams College before rejoining his

Secretary of State James Blaine supports the wounded President as bystanders grab his assailant. Washington, D. C., July 2, 1881. Garfield's assassin, Charles Guiteau, had a long history of failures capped by Blaine's refusal to make him an ambassador. Though Guiteau was probably insane, he was convicted by a jury and was hanged in 1882.

family at Elberon. As he waited for a train, a man in the crowded station fired two shots, grazing Garfield's arm and hitting him in the back. The man shouted, "I am a Stalwart and Arthur is President now!"

Garfield lived through the long summer of 1881, as doctors searched for the hidden bullet. Lucretia helped nurse him and cooked many of his meals. In September he said that he wanted to go to Elberon for the sea air. He was taken there on a train which ran on special tracks right up to their cottage. On September 19 he died.

Friends of the Garfields raised a fund of money to support Lucretia and her family.

## Ellen Herndon Arthur
(1837-1880)

Ellen Herndon was born in Fredericksburg, Virginia. Her father was a naval officer. On a visit to New York she met Chester Alan Arthur, a Vermonter by birth, and member of a New York City law firm. They were married in 1859 and had three children, one of whom died as a baby.

Soon after their marriage, Arthur began his rapid climb in the Republican party of New York State. During the Civil War he was appointed to outfit the New York militia. After the war he worked with Senator Roscoe Conkling to build up the Republican machine in New York. As Conkling's right-hand man, he was appointed Collector of the Port of New York by President Grant. In this post he was to take charge of collecting taxes on imported goods. It was assumed that he would spend a good part of his time assigning party workers to the many jobs in the customs office. He performed both tasks with efficiency.

In 1878 President Hayes, in a move to unscramble government workers from party workers, asked Arthur to resign. Roscoe Conkling put up resistance in the Senate, but it did no good. Arthur left the customs house in 1879.

The Arthurs were active in New York society and both were fond of elegant clothing, decoration, and manners. Ellen had a beautiful voice and often sang at programs given by the rich for the benefit of charity. After singing at a charity program early in January 1880, she caught a cold. Three days later she died of pneumonia.

Ellen Arthur did not live to become First Lady. During his presidency Arthur put fresh flowers by her picture every day.

Chester Alan Arthur
(1830-1886)

Six months after her death, Arthur was nominated for Vice-President to run with Garfield. His nomination was Roscoe Conkling's last major achievement. After the election Conkling and Arthur tangled with President Garfield over the New York appointments. In September 1881, after Garfield's death, Arthur became President. He had spent a grim summer. Most people expected — and feared — that the White House would become a haven for Roscoe Conkling and the New York crowd.

Arthur fooled everybody. As President he governed with honesty and efficiency, and he supported civil service reform. Driven to it by Garfield's assassination, Congress

Mary Arthur McElroy came to Washington each winter for the social season and helped care for Arthur's daughter Nell.

passed the Pendleton Civil Service Act which provided for a merit system for certain government jobs (a list which was lengthened in later years).

Arthur probably surprised nobody at all in his management of the White House. "It looks like a badly kept barracks," he said as he ordered designer Louis Comfort Tiffany to make some improvements. Tiffany took charge of a crew of painters during the autumn of 1881, and in December Arthur moved in. A French chef prepared his meals, and his sister, Mary Arthur McElroy, came down from Albany to act as hostess.

By 1884 the Stalwarts had deserted Arthur and he had found no group of supporters to replace them. James Blaine was nominated for President and a Democrat won.

# Frances Folsom Cleveland
(1864-1947)

Frances Folsom was born in Buffalo, New York, where her father, Oscar Folsom, was a law partner of Grover Cleveland. When Frances was 11 her father died and Cleveland became her guardian. Frances went to Wells College, and Cleveland sent her letters and flowers. After her graduation in 1885 he helped her plan a trip to Europe.

Cleveland had been active in the Democratic party during the 1860's and 1870's, serving Erie County as assistant district attorney and sheriff. In 1881, backed by reform Democrats, he became mayor of Buffalo, and surprised his supporters by outdoing their demands for reform. He was elected governor of New York a year later.

By 1884 the Republican reputation for corrupt government had become too much for most people, including a number of Republicans. These were the *mugwumps*. When James Blaine was nominated for President they left the Republican convention and offered to support a reform Democrat. The Democratic party got the message. They nominated Cleveland. After a bitter campaign Cleveland won by a slim margin.

Frances Cleveland. The President always called her by her nickname, Frank.

Grover Cleveland
(1837-1908)

Cleveland was the first Democrat elected President since Buchanan, and like Buchanan he was not married when he entered the White House. He asked his sister Rose to come down from New York to act as hostess. Rose had lectured at girls' schools, and her scholarly manner frightened some of the congressional wives. She suited Cleveland well enough, though he did not permit her to stop serving wine at White House dinners. In June 1886 Rose went back to New York, and Cleveland sent out hand-written invitations to his wedding.

A White House wedding: President Cleveland and Frances
Folsom were married in the Blue Room on June 2, 1886.

Frances Folsom, with her mother, arrived in Washington on June 2. All day florists filled the Blue Room with
roses and pansies. That evening John Philip Sousa and the
Marine Band played the wedding march as Frances and
the President came down the stairs. Frances drew her
15-foot train into the Blue Room without losing her balance
or knocking anything over.

The Clevelands went to the Maryland shore for a honeymoon. They were followed by newsmen with spyglasses. Later Cleveland attacked them in a letter to the New York papers, but press and public alike refused to lose interest in the young First Lady. People mobbed the White House receptions. On one occasion several women, straining for another look at Frances, crashed into a row of potted palms.

Benjamin Harrison held the White House from 1889 until 1893 when the Clevelands returned for a second term. To escape the curious eye of the public they kept away from the White House as much as possible; they had a farm near Washington, and after 1893 spent much of their time at a rented house in the suburbs. Every summer they vacationed in Maine. The Clevelands had five children. Their second daughter, Esther, the first and last President's child born in the White House, lived until 1980.

The chief issues throughout Cleveland's presidency—besides civil service reform—were economic. The problems of gold and silver, high tariffs and low, labor and business and farming all became more critical early in his second term when a financial panic broke out.

During the panic, Cleveland's doctors found that he had developed a cancer of the mouth and decided they had to operate. To keep the stock market from plunging further, Cleveland decided to keep his operation a secret. With his doctors he boarded a yacht in New York harbor. As the boat turned up the East River, the doctors removed his left upper jaw. Cleveland recovered completely and later wore a rubber jaw.

Cleveland was a reformer of government practices but he usually took a conservative, Eastern, sound-money stand on most issues. By 1896 the more radical, Middle Western farming wing of the party took control and nominated William Jennings Bryan for the presidency. Cleveland did not campaign for Bryan. In March 1897 the Republican winner, William McKinley, dined at the White House with the Clevelands the night before his inauguration.

With his family Cleveland moved to Princeton, New Jersey, where he lectured at the university and became a friend of Woodrow Wilson. Cleveland died in 1908. Five years later Frances married Thomas J. Preston, Jr., a professor at Princeton. Her fans continued to call her Mrs. Cleveland.

# Caroline Scott Harrison
(1832-1892)

Caroline Scott was born in Oxford, Ohio. She met Benjamin Harrison when he came from North Bend, Ohio, to attend Farmers' College near Cincinnati. A year younger than Caroline, Harrison was the grandson of President William Henry Harrison. He graduated from Miami University in Oxford, and in 1853 he and Caroline were married. Within a year they moved to Indianapolis, a growing frontier town. There he set up a law office and became active in city politics and the Republican party. Caroline had two children, Russell and Mary.

The Civil War interrupted Harrison's law career. He recruited the 70th Regiment of Indiana Volunteers, which was sent to Tennessee and Kentucky for guard duty before joining General Sherman in Georgia. During the war Caroline visited Harrison at camp and helped nurse his men. "Little Ben"— as he was called by his troops — left the army a brigadier general.

Caroline Harrison

Benjamin Harrison
(1833-1901)

Back in Indiana, Harrison worked as a corporation lawyer and made an unsuccessful try for the governorship. In 1881 he was elected to the United States Senate, and his family moved to Washington. Facing a Democratic state legislature in 1886, he lost a bid for re-election by one vote.

The Republicans nominated Harrison for President in 1888 and campaigned with the song "Grandfather's Hat Fits Ben." Harrison made speeches from his front porch to visiting delegations. He supported a high tariff, and President Cleveland, who did not campaign, favored a reduced tariff. Harrison got 90,000 fewer popular votes than Cleveland but more votes in the Electoral College.

Russell Harrison with the Harrison grandchildren and pets on the White House lawn. Baby McKee holds the reins.

Cleveland went back to New York and in March 1889 the Harrisons moved into the White House. They were joined by Caroline's father and her widowed niece, Mrs. Mary Scott Dimmick, who acted as her secretary. Russell and Mary brought their families to live in the White House too. Nellie Grant's old room became a nursery for three babies. One of them was Benjamin Harrison McKee, Mary's son, who was universally known as Baby McKee. Word went out that Baby McKee was at his grandfather's elbow day and night. Actually, the little boy spent most of his time with his sister Mary and cousin Marthena.

Caroline Harrison felt that the White House was much too small for her family. She supervised an architect who drew up three new plans for the house. His third plan, the most ambitious, added two huge wings, joined on the south side by a long row of greenhouses. A later plan drawn up during the second Cleveland term tripled the length of the house. None of the plans was carried out.

A White House office newly wired for electricity, 1891.

Caroline did make changes inside the house. A new method of rat control was undertaken, and new floors were laid. In 1891 the first electric lights and doorbells were installed. The Harrisons worried about the new lights. Afraid of shock, they often used the old gas-lights, and sometimes they ordered a brave electrician to turn the lights on and off. Caroline also set up the first White House Christmas tree for her grandson Baby McKee.

Harrison was renominated in 1892, to run against Cleveland as well as a third party, the Populists, made up chiefly of farmers who felt neglected by the Eastern wings of both parties. Two weeks before the election Caroline Harrison died. Defeated by Cleveland, Harrison went back to Indianapolis. In 1896 he married Mary Dimmick, Caroline's niece.

## Ida Saxton McKinley
(1847-1907)

Ida Saxton was born in Canton, Ohio. Her banker father believed in women's rights. Ida received a good education and traveled in Europe before returning to Ohio to become a clerk in her father's bank.

William McKinley came to Canton to set up his law practice in 1867. He met Ida, and they were married in 1871. During the first five years of their marriage they had two daughters, Katherine and Ida, both of whom died as small children. Ida's mother died in 1873. Shocked and grieved by the three deaths, she was to be ill for the rest of her life. Epilepsy, a disease of the nervous system, made her often weak and a victim of blackouts. McKinley took good care of his wife and gave her every possible thoughtful attention.

In 1876 McKinley, a Republican, was elected to the House of Representatives. Except for one term, he remained in the House until 1891. He supported increased coinage of silver and a high tariff, and thus pleased both farmers and industrialists. In 1888 the McKinley Tariff Act raised taxes on imports to a new high. McKinley was not re-elected in the 1890 election, and in 1892 his tariff was still a major issue, helping President Harrison lose his office to Cleveland.

Meanwhile, McKinley had caught the eye of Ohio industrialist Mark Hanna. Hanna's money and his political machine helped McKinley to the governorship in 1891 and again in 1893. During legislative sessions in Columbus, the McKinleys stayed in a hotel across the street from the state house. Every morning Governor McKinley bowed to

Ida from the state house steps, and at 3 p.m. he left his work and waved to her from the window.

Hanna's McKinley-for-President campaign began in 1892. Harrison got the nomination, but by 1896 Hanna's money and strategy succeeded. McKinley was nominated on the first ballot and faced the Democrat William Jennings Bryan. During the campaign, McKinley would not leave his wife, so Hanna rounded up great crowds of people and brought them to McKinley. The candidate spoke to them from his flag-draped front porch in Canton, Ohio. Bryan campaigned for free coinage of silver, so McKinley switched from silver to gold, which suited industrialist Hanna's platform better anyway. The choice between the parties was clear-cut. McKinley won with ease.

Because of Ida's illness, President McKinley kept White House life as simple as possible. Cousins and nieces took charge of party-giving and one of them usually acted as hostess. Ida stayed in an upstairs sitting room where she sewed for charity and embroidered for pleasure. She and McKinley often went for long rides in their carriage. Unless she felt very ill, she usually came to state dinners, where if she had an attack, she was careful never to faint. McKinley seated her next to himself instead of at the other end of the table.

William McKinley (1843-1901)

Ida relied entirely upon her husband for company, but early in his term trouble with Spain kept McKinley in his office and map room most of the time. For 30 years Cuba had struggled for freedom from Spain, and by the mid-nineties American interest in the island had become intense. Lively, semi-fictional reports in the newspapers made many Americans look upon Cuba with pity and an eagerness bordering on greed. McKinley was urged to declare war on Spain. For a year he held back. On February

15, 1898, an American gunboat, the U.S.S. *Maine,* was blown up in Havana harbor. Nobody knew who did it, but everybody assumed it was Spain. In April McKinley asked Congress to declare war. Four months later the Spanish-American War was over, with the Spanish navy defeated in Santiago harbor, and for good measure, in Manila Bay. America's involvement in world politics dates from this time.

McKinley was re-elected in 1900, again defeating Bryan. In September 1901, six months after his inauguration, he and Ida went to the Pan-American Exposition in Buffalo, New York. McKinley gave a speech which hinted strongly that he was about to lower the tariff. The next day, September 6, McKinley went to a public reception at the Temple of Music. As he shook hands with the crowd, he was shot twice by an anarchist, Leon Czolgosz, whose gun was hidden under a handkerchief.

A week later McKinley died. Ida did not return to the White House. She went home to Canton, where she died in 1907.

Edith Roosevelt

## Edith Carow Roosevelt

(1861-1948)

Edith Carow was born in Norwich, Connecticut, of socially prominent and wealthy parents. Edith and Theodore Roosevelt knew each other from childhood. In 1880 Roosevelt graduated from Harvard and that fall he married Alice Hathaway Lee. For a short time he studied law at Columbia University but he found his classes boring. Though his friends in society looked down upon politics, he joined the Republican party and ran for the state assembly in 1881. The other legislators laughed at his sideburns and fine clothes. He was considered a dandy, but he worked hard and was re-elected twice. Under Democratic governor Grover Cleveland he developed an interest in government reform.

On February 14, 1884, Alice died, two days after giving birth to a daughter. His mother, ill with typhoid fever, died the same day. Roosevelt put aside his political activities in New York and went west to be a rancher in the Dakota territory. There he lived the rough life. Some days he spent 12 to 16 hours in the saddle, tending his herds. Out of the saddle, he wrote books. He also wrote letters to his old friend Edith Carow, and on trips east he visited her.

During the winter of 1885-1886 most of his cattle were killed by heavy snows. Roosevelt moved back to New York City, and on December 2, 1886, he and Edith were married in London. They went to live at Sagamore Hill, Roosevelt's home in Oyster Bay, Long Island. Edith had five children — Theodore, Jr., Kermit, Ethel, Archie, and Quentin — and she also raised young Alice, the daughter of Roosevelt's first wife.

Roosevelt lost a bid to be mayor of New York in 1886 but he was clearly back in politics. He campaigned for Harrison in 1888, and after the election was appointed a Civil Service Commissioner. In 1895 he headed New York's Board of Police Commissioners and in 1897 became McKinley's Assistant Secretary of the Navy.

One of Roosevelt's favorite sports was the obstacle hike, a long tramp of several miles in which one was to jump over anything — including a mountain — that got in one's way. In politics too, he made his way by leaping over and diving under the dominant forces in his party. His reform measures were opposed by the conservative businessmen who ran the Republican party, but these same measures made them put him up for office. They knew that a reform candidate could win votes.

So could a military hero. When the Spanish-American War broke out in 1898, Roosevelt resigned his position, rounded up a cavalry unit — the Rough Riders — and hurried to Cuba. On July 1 he led a charge up San Juan Hill, near Santiago. After the war Republican leaders in New York grabbed Roosevelt for the governorship and then in 1900 they nominated him for Vice-President with McKinley in order to get him out of New York.

President and Vice-President were both in New York when McKinley was shot on September 6, 1901. On the 13th, Roosevelt was climbing in the Adirondacks when a messenger notified him that McKinley was dying. He reached Buffalo at dawn on the 14th, a few hours after the President's death.

That fall the White House became noisier than it had ever been. The younger Roosevelts roller-skated in the upstairs hall, threw spitballs at the portrait of Andrew Jackson, and leaped over chairs in the reception rooms. When he had time, Roosevelt joined them, though he preferred tennis and boxing. Calm Edith Roosevelt let them do as they liked. She governed her family more closely at the dinner table, watching their elbows and their conversation. Prize-fighting, she felt, was not a suitable subject at mealtime.

Theodore Roosevelt (1858-1919) with his family at Sagamore Hill, 1903: (left to right) Quentin, the President, Theodore, Jr., Archie, Alice, Kermit, Edith, and Ethel.

Edith's own upbringing had provided her with a set of unbreakable moral and social rules, and people who broke them were not invited to the White House. Every Tuesday morning the Cabinet wives sat down with her in the Green Room to knit and embroider and talk about the more interesting examples of bad behavior.

At White House parties, Edith greeted her guests with charm and ease. Sensibly, she had cut down her work beforehand by hiring a social secretary—the first in the White House—and a caterer to serve at formal dinners. Enlargement of the White House made things easier too. During the summer of 1902 the family moved to a house on Lafayette Square while workmen tore down the greenhouses and built a neat one-story wing on each side of the house. Offices were moved from the second floor to the west wing, leaving extra space upstairs for the family. New systems of plumbing, heating, and electricity were installed, and Chester Alan Arthur's splendid old Tiffany screen was torn out of the entrance hall. The Roosevelts liked simplicity.

Alice Roosevelt, who made her debut in 1902, was an elegant and sharp-witted young lady. Newsmen referred to her as "Princess Alice" and reported to the nation everything that she did or said. In February 1906 she married Representative Nicholas Longworth of Ohio. Her wedding in the East Room was the biggest Washington event since Nellie Grant's marriage in 1874. Alice had fewer flowers than Nellie, and only one attendant—her father. After the wedding she began to slice her cake. It was tedious work, so she borrowed a sword from a military man and finished the job with that. (Nicholas died in 1936 but Alice, who never remarried, remained a lively member of Washington society until her death at age 96. In his 1980 eulogy for her, President Jimmy Carter said that the outspoken Alice personified the freshness and irreverence of modern times.)

Roosevelt brought a similar sweeping energy to his work as President. Under Cleveland and Harrison Congress had passed laws regulating big business—the Interstate Commerce Act and the Sherman Anti-Trust Act—but these laws had remained untouched by human hands. Roosevelt began to enforce them by bringing suit against the larger trusts, and he had Congress add other measures to protect the consumer and the country's natural resources. Long a believer in sea power, Roosevelt built up the Navy and sent it on a good-will trip around the world. People everywhere cheered the big white ships, and Roosevelt assumed his message was not lost.

In 1908 Roosevelt (who had won a second term in 1904) asked the party to nominate his Secretary of War, William Howard Taft. The next spring, with Taft safely in the White House, Roosevelt took his family back to Sagamore Hill and went to Africa to hunt big game.

## Helen Herron Taft
(1861-1943)

Helen Herron was born in Cincinnati, Ohio. Her father, John W. Herron, was a law partner of Rutherford B. Hayes. Helen studied in private schools and became an accomplished pianist. In 1886 she married William

Howard Taft, the lawyer son of Alphonso Taft, a power in the Republican party. The Tafts had three children, Robert, Helen, and Charles.

A graduate of Yale University and Cincinnati Law School, Taft had a successful law practice, and had held several legal positions in Hamilton County. In 1887 he was appointed judge of the superior court in Cincinnati. Taft was happiest as a lawyer and judge. He did not like politics. But his family was active in the Republican party, and his wife was a clever woman with political interest and skill. She advised Taft and urged him to seek office. Two appointments in the 1890's gave Taft the kind of work he liked to do, though they seemed at the moment to side-track Helen's ambitions. In 1890 Benjamin Harrison named him United States Solicitor General, and in 1892 he gave Taft a federal judgeship on the Circuit Court of Appeals.

After the war with Spain, the Philippine Islands became a United States territory. In 1900 President McKinley sent Taft to the islands to help organize a colonial government. The next year Taft was appointed governor. Helen and the children joined him in Manila. Taft was an excellent governor and his family enjoyed life in the exotic East.

They moved to Washington in 1904 when Taft became Roosevelt's Secretary of War. Taft's department directed work on the Panama Canal, and he helped Roosevelt settle the Russo-Japanese War. In 1908, at Roosevelt's recommendation, the Republicans nominated Taft for the presidency. He defeated William Jennings Bryan, the Democrats' constant candidate, in his third and last presidential campaign.

After the inauguration Roosevelt parted from the Tafts on the Capitol steps. He had decided not to ride to the White House with the new President, and his carriage space was free for Helen Taft, who was glad to take it. She looked forward to the presidency. Taft did not.

Helen was a practiced hostess after years of experience in the Philippines and as a Cabinet wife. She hired a housekeeper to replace the male steward, because she was sure that a woman could do a better job. Oriental furniture went into the Oval Room to remind the Tafts of the Philippines, and a new Victor talking machine was installed in the Blue Room. On warm summer nights the President and his wife sat on the south portico and listened to records. The family cow, Pauline Wayne, grazed on the lawn near the old State Department.

Taft's bathtub

Helen Taft did two great favors for the city of Washington. In the Philippines she had discovered the outdoor bandstand, and at her suggestion a stand was built in Potomac Park so that Washingtonians could cool off at a concert. Taft appeared on horseback at the grand opening of the new bandstand. Helen's second gift was also from the Orient. She negotiated with the mayor of Tokyo for a shipload of cherry trees to be planted near the Capitol and on the rim of the Tidal Basin.

During her first year in the White House Helen Taft had a slight stroke. Weakened by illness, she could no longer be a full-time hostess. Her sisters and her daughter Helen often helped Taft at official functions.

William Howard Taft (1857-1930)

Taft himself was neither a great political manager nor a showman, and he knew it. Reporters waited in vain for clever phrases, and Roosevelt's followers decided that Taft was not being true to the progressive cause. Conservatives in Congress got the upper hand and unlike Roosevelt, Taft did not fight back. His administration broke up more trusts than Roosevelt's, but setbacks in conservation and another high tariff made the liberals angry. In June 1910 Roosevelt came back from Africa. He found the party badly cracked. It broke in 1912.

Roosevelt entered and won several state primaries, but the Republican convention nominated Taft. The progressives left the convention and formed a third party, the Bull Moose. People sang "Get on the raft with Taft, boys," but Taft came in third, behind the winner Wilson and the Bull Moose Roosevelt. Ex-President Taft taught law at Yale University until 1921 when he became Chief Justice of the Supreme Court, the job he had really wanted all along.

## Ellen Axson Wilson

(1860-1914)

Ellen Axson was born in Savannah, Georgia. She was
the daughter of a Presbyterian minister. Ellen loved to
draw and wanted to become an artist. She met Woodrow
Wilson in 1883 when he came to Georgia on a business
trip. Wilson, also a minister's son, was born in Staunton,
Virginia, and grew up in Georgia and South Carolina. He

graduated from Princeton University in 1879, studied and practiced law for a short time, and then decided to become a teacher. When he met Ellen, he was a graduate student in history and politics at Johns Hopkins University in Baltimore. They were married in June 1885 and that fall went to live at Bryn Mawr, Pennsylvania. Wilson taught history at Bryn Mawr College and later at Wesleyan University in Connecticut, where he also coached a winning football team. The Wilsons had three daughters—Margaret, Jessie, and Eleanor. Wilson liked to play games with them. He made up funny stories and read aloud to them from the novels of Dickens and Scott.

In 1890 Wilson became a professor at Princeton University. Twelve years later, in 1902, he became president of the school. Wilson worked to strengthen the school as a place of learning rather than a social center. He enraged many of the old graduates, and by 1910 was ready to accept an offer to run for governor of New Jersey. The corrupt Democratic party needed a clean and honest candidate; Wilson was elected, and began to clean up New Jersey. His reforms were both political and social, and by 1912 he was clearly part of the progressive movement emerging in both parties. At their Baltimore convention the Democrats nominated Wilson for President on the 46th ballot. He defeated Roosevelt and Taft, and in March 1913 his family moved into the White House.

The Wilsons didn't give an inaugural ball. They were not fond of big parties, and later, Ellen Wilson would often sit in silence through an entire dinner. She was, however, a warm and tactful person.

Woodrow Wilson (1856-1924) with Ellen and daughters Margaret, Eleanor, and Jessie, on the lawn at Princeton, 1912.

Ellen liked books and art and shared with her daughters an interest in social work. She took members of Congress on a walk through Washington and showed them what needed to be done. Her quiet influence resulted in a slum clearance bill for the city.

Ellen Wilson's greatest efforts of feeling, thought, and activity were directed toward her husband. Accordingly, she felt that the White House itself should be a comfortable home, not primarily an auditorium, reception hall, or museum. The Wilsons avoided the family dining room because they disliked its dark heavy furniture. In the State Dining Room they did not want to dine under the hairy heads mounted by Theodore Roosevelt after his hunting trips, so they pulled a table to the far end of the room and ate looking out upon the White House gardens.

Jessie Wilson was married in the White House in November 1913. Not long after Eleanor's wedding in the spring of 1914, Ellen Wilson became ill. She died on August 6, 1914—two days after the German invasion of Belgium. Wilson sank into deep despair.

## Edith Bolling Galt Wilson
(1872-1961)

Edith Bolling was born in Wytheville, Virginia. In 1896 she married Norman Galt, a jeweler in Washington, D.C. Galt died two years after their marriage. Edith met Woodrow Wilson in March 1915. The President sent her flowers and took her for rides in his motor. In late April Wilson proposed marriage, and in September Edith agreed.

His aides protested, claiming that so swift a remarriage would be bad for the 1916 election. Wilson with some difficulty was able to overrule them. He and Edith Galt were married in her home on December 18, 1915.

Edith was a gay and charming woman, and a good companion for Wilson. She was also intelligent and firm-willed. Historians still argue about her role in Wilson's presidency, especially during the last years.

During Wilson's first term Congress enacted strong reforms in banking, business, and the tariff, but after 1914 Wilson's greatest problem was World War I. In 1914 the Germans had expected to capture Paris within a month. Instead a long battle line formed from Belgium down through northeastern France, and four years of bitter trench warfare began. At sea, German submarines attacked British ships. They also hit neutral America's merchant vessels, and eventually drew the United States into the war. On April 2, 1917, Wilson asked Congress to declare war on Germany. In June the first American forces landed in France with General Pershing.

At the White House, Edith Wilson set up her sewing machine in an upstairs room and began to turn out pajamas and hospital shirts for the soldiers. A vegetable garden was planted on the White House grounds, and a large flock of sheep grazed on the lawn. Their wool at auction provided $100,000 for the Red Cross.

The war ended with an armistice in November 1918, and a month later Edith traveled with Wilson to the Paris Peace Conference. Later, when it appeared that the Senate would reject the peace treaty and with it the League of Nations, Wilson went on a speaking tour to urge support for the League. He rushed by train from one western town to another. The trip was exhausting. Wilson collapsed and went back to Washington. A few days later, on October 3, 1919, he had a stroke from which he never completely recovered.

Edith helped nurse him during his long illness, and for the rest of his term she acted as a go-between, bringing him news and lists of problems and helping him sign documents. For nearly 18 months the White House gates were locked to the public.

The Senate did not ratify the peace treaty and the United States never joined the League. In December 1920, a month after the election of Warren Harding, Wilson was given a Nobel prize for peace. In March 1921 the Wilsons went to live in a house on S Street in Washington, D.C., where he died in 1924.

Florence Harding. Her husband called her "the Duchess."

## Florence Kling DeWolfe Harding
(1860-1924)

Florence Kling was born in Marion, Ohio. Her banker father provided her with a good education. She taught music until her marriage to Henry DeWolfe. The marriage was an unhappy one, and after a divorce Florence returned to her father's home with her son.

Warren Gamelial Harding had come to Marion from Corsica, Ohio, with his parents in 1882, at the age of 17. A few years later with some friends he bought the bank-rupt *Marion Star,* and in 1891 he married Florence Kling DeWolfe. For 14 years Florence helped with the newspaper, riding a bicycle to and from work. As circulation manager she made the old weekly paper a thriving daily. Warren Harding, editor and publisher, became a pillar of the church, a noted businessman, and a friend to local politicians. He was a Republican.

In 1898 he was elected to the state senate, and in 1903 he became lieutenant governor of Ohio. He tried for the governorship in 1910 but lost. In 1912 the party chose him to nominate Taft for re-election. Harding later said that this was one of the bigger thrills of his life.

Florence Harding was an ambitious woman. With the backing of Harding's friend, Ohio political boss Harry M. Daugherty, she urged her husband to run for the United

Warren G. Harding (1865-1923)

States Senate in 1914, and later for the presidency. Senator Harding was not very interested in political issues or in legislation, but he worked hard to help his friends. At the Republican convention in 1920, the party was torn between three candidates, none of whom could get enough votes for nomination. Harry Daugherty called a meeting in what he termed a "smoke-filled room," and his guests decided to nominate Harding. Governor Calvin Coolidge of Massachusetts completed the ticket.

The Republican platform opposed the League of Nations, and Harding from his front porch promised a return to "normalcy," a word which he coined. Harding and Coolidge easily defeated the Democratic candidate, Governor James Cox of Ohio, and his running mate Franklin D. Roosevelt.

The Hardings moved into the White House and had the gates unlocked so that the public could again visit the building. The years of war and illness were over, and the Hardings gave many parties. The 18th Amendment, ratified in 1919, kept wine out of the State Dining Room, but upstairs Harding's guests could have whatever they liked.

Florence Harding gave large garden parties and small dinner parties. Surrounded by dignitaries she planted a tree on the White House lawn. She greeted Camp Fire Girls and entertained wounded veterans of the war. She also helped Harding pick government officials. Many of them were old friends from Ohio.

From the White House steps, Florence Harding sends a pigeon to a poultry show.

In the summer of 1923 Harding went on a long speaking tour. With Florence, a number of assistants, and a great deal of luggage he traveled across the country and up to Canada and Alaska. On the return trip down the west coast Harding received a long coded message from Washington. The Senate, he was told, was investigating some government oil leases. By the time his train reached San Francisco, Harding was very ill. He was taken to a hotel where he died on August 2.

A funeral train took Harding and his party back to Washington. Florence Harding burned every letter she could find, and went back to Marion, Ohio, where she died in 1924. Attorney General Harry Daugherty, accused of conspiring to defraud the government, stood trial and was freed when two juries could not agree on a verdict. Even before Harding's death scandals had been unearthed in the Veterans' Bureau and in the Departments of Justice and the Interior. The public did not hear of them until further investigations and trials were conducted. For nearly a decade the daily news was spotted with reminders of the Harding years. One of the most interesting was the Teapot Dome oil scandal. Secretary of the Interior Albert Fall had leased government oil lands at Teapot Dome, Wyoming, to private oilmen. He had received large gifts for his favors. Harry Daugherty was involved in Teapot Dome too, and he was well informed about other government activities. He wrote a book about them in 1932.

Grace Coolidge had two sons, one of whom died during the
summer of 1924, at the age of 16.

## Grace Goodhue Coolidge
(1879-1957)

Grace Goodhue was born in Burlington, Vermont. She
graduated from the University of Vermont in 1902 and
taught for three years at the Clarke School for the Deaf in
Northampton, Massachusetts. In Northampton she met

Calvin Coolidge, another Vermonter. A graduate of Amherst College, he was a lawyer and a Republican, and had already been in and out of several city offices. They were married in 1905. Their sons John and Calvin, Jr., were born in 1906 and 1908.

Coolidge held several state offices before his nomination for the vice-presidency in 1920. He was a member of the Massachusetts legislature, mayor of Northampton, and lieutenant governor of the state. He first attracted national attention in 1919 when, as a governor of Massachusetts, he called in the state guard to halt a strike of policemen in Boston.

When Harding died, Coolidge was at his father's farm in Vermont. At 2:45 in the morning his father gave him the oath of office. The new President went back to bed and slept until morning. Later Attorney General Daugherty, concerned about the finer points of law, made him take the oath again in Washington.

Grace Coolidge had become familiar with Washington society as wife of the Vice-President and she easily took on her new responsibilities. As White House hostess she was an effective counter-balance to the host. Coolidge was shy and silent, a man of few words. Grace, on the other hand, was lively and talkative. People delighted her. Photographs of Grace Coolidge reveal an impish face: a wide mouth and curious eyes amused by what they see.

Although Grace did not pry into political matters or give her husband tips about running the government, he took a great interest in the White House kitchen, nosing in and out of the ice boxes, budget notebooks, and menus. Though a thrifty man (in government and in private life) he liked to buy exotic dresses and hats for his wife. She usually managed to avoid wearing these beaded, fringed, and flowered garments.

Coolidge himself had avoided connections with the corrupt members of Harding's government. Most of them were brought to court during his presidency. In 1924 Harry Daugherty was asked to resign.

Coolidge's government on the whole did not interfere with anything—business was allowed to run wild and farming to run dry; the tariff remained high and the immigration quota low. He was easily elected to a term of his own in 1924, defeating the Democrat John W. Davis and a third party candidate, Progressive Robert M. LaFollette.

During the summer of 1927, while the White House roof was being fixed, the Coolidges took a vacation in the Black Hills. On August 2, in Rapid City, South Dakota, Coolidge told reporters, "I do not choose to run for President in 1928." Actually he did not go so far as to speak these words. He wrote them on slips of paper which he handed to each reporter. The Republican party, though surprised, followed his wishes and nominated Herbert Hoover.

Calvin Coolidge (1872-1933) with Grace and Rob Roy.

The Coolidges went back to Northampton. To escape from curious tourists they bought an estate called The Beeches, where Coolidge wrote his autobiography and a daily newspaper column. In October 1929 the stock market crashed and the Depression followed. Coolidge became sad and confused and thought perhaps he was partly to blame. In January 1933 he died of a heart attack. Grace Coolidge sold the estate. She lived in Northampton until her death in 1957.

## Lou Henry Hoover

(1875-1944)

Lou Henry was born in Waterloo, Iowa. Her father was a wealthy banker who moved his family to Monterey, California. Lou met Herbert Hoover in a geology lab at Stanford University. He was also an Iowan, an orphan who had gone west at the age of 11 to live with an uncle in Oregon. In 1891 he had entered the first class at Stanford. He planned to become a mining engineer. He and Lou became engaged but agreed to wait for marriage until he had tried his hand at mining.

For two years Hoover worked in Australia, managing gold mines for an English company. In 1899 he got a new job — in China — and wired a definite proposal to Lou Henry. They were married in Monterey and sailed the next day for China. Lou was a bright young woman with scholarly interests, and she made good use of her time in China. While Hoover went inland to search for new mines and to run the old ones, she learned to speak Chinese and began to collect Chinese porcelain.

After the Boxer Rebellion of 1900 the Chinese Imperial Bureau of Mines folded up, and Hoover began to travel and to work for other companies. As his mining activities spread round the world Hoover became wealthy. By 1908 he was centered in London with his own firm. Lou's sons Herbert, Jr., and Allan were born in London. In their spare time the Hoovers translated into English a Latin text on mining published in 1556.

The Hoovers were in London when World War I broke out. During the war years Hoover turned his engineering skills to the task of moving people and food from one place to another. In 1914 he sent 120,000 Americans home from Europe and began to organize relief for Belgium. When

America entered the war in 1917 Hoover was asked to direct the United States Food Administration. Americans learned to *Hooverize* — to eat less in order to save food for starving Europeans.

During the twenties Hoover was Secretary of Commerce under Harding and Coolidge, and in 1928 the Republicans nominated him for President. Hoover campaigned for "two chickens in every pot" and beat the Democratic candidate, Governor Alfred E. Smith of New York. Hoover carried 40 of the 48 states.

When Lou Hoover moved into the White House, the decor changed. Art objects collected on her travels appeared in every room. In the upstairs hallway, bamboo chairs and grass rugs were arranged beneath a huge canary cage. Lou became a much admired hostess. She gave many parties and always had company for dinner — sometimes more than she bargained for. Once, 500 people turned up for dinner when the Hoovers had expected 200. White House maids ran to the neighborhood stores to pick up more food. With a little Hooverizing they were able to serve the crowd.

When Hoover had time, he liked to fish at his camp in the Blue Ridge Mountains. Lou served as president of the Girl Scouts and lent help to many of her husband's relief programs.

But things did not go smoothly for long. Seven months after Hoover's inauguration, the stock market crashed. People lost money, jobs, and homes. The Hoover adminis-

Herbert Hoover (1874-1964) and Lou with Herbert, Jr., his wife, and Allan.

tration tried to help by offering relief to drought victims, setting up a federal farm board, and making loans to keep industries afloat. But by 1932, 10 million people were out of work.

In 1932 Hoover was renominated for President. But voters blamed the Republicans for the worsening Depression, and Democrat Franklin Roosevelt won the election. After his defeat, Hoover spent a lot of time writing and speaking. He and Lou moved to New York City, where Lou died on January 7, 1944. Hoover continued to lead an active life until the age of 90. He died in 1964 in New York.

Eleanor Roosevelt, July 1933

## Anna Eleanor Roosevelt
(1884-1962)

Eleanor Roosevelt was born in New York City. Her father was a younger brother of Theodore Roosevelt. Both her parents died when she was a child and at 10 she went to live with her grandmother in upstate New York. Eleanor was a shy girl whose family nickname was "Granny." She studied with tutors and at 15 went abroad to attend a private school near London. In 1902, at the age of 18, she sailed back to New York where she made her debut in society. She was almost six feet tall and still very shy.

Eleanor had known Franklin Roosevelt (a fifth cousin) since childhood, but only slightly. In 1903 when he graduated from Harvard they became engaged. Then Roosevelt told his mother. Sara Roosevelt did not like the idea at all. She took her son off to the Caribbean on a vacation, confident that he would be distracted enough to change his plans. She didn't succeed.

Franklin and Eleanor Roosevelt were married in 1905. Eleanor's uncle, the President, gave her away. Sara Roosevelt continued her attempted takeover, renting and furnishing a house for them. The situation was probably not easy for Eleanor, but she did not make a fuss. She was very busy.

The Roosevelts had six children. Anna Eleanor, born in 1906, was followed by five younger brothers, one of whom died in infancy. Roosevelt worked in a law firm but was bored until he ran for the state senate in 1910. A Democrat, he won election in a long-time Republican district and became active in the progressive wing of his party. In the 1912 election he did not support cousin Theodore. President Wilson appointed him Assistant Secretary of the Navy. Roosevelt loved boats and naval history, and from his boss, Navy Secretary Josephus Daniels, he learned about politics. In the 1920 election he was the Democratic candidate for Vice-President, with James Cox — a throwaway election because everybody knew Harding would win.

In 1921, during a summer vacation at Campobello Island near New Brunswick, Canada, Roosevelt had an attack of polio which crippled him. He was in terrible pain on and off for many months. His hands, arms, and back recovered with time and exercise; and with leg braces and crutches he learned to walk. During these months Eleanor began to help him politically. Sara Roosevelt wanted her son to retire to the family home at Hyde Park, but Eleanor and Roosevelt's secretary Louis Howe argued for the political life. Eleanor had been involved in social causes since the days of her engagement when she taught gym and dancing in a New York settlement house, but before 1921 she cared little for politics. Now, with Louis Howe's coaching she learned to speak well and to fight down her shyness.

Franklin D. Roosevelt (1882-1945) returns
to Washington from a vacation, 1934.

She went to political meetings, listened and watched, and
reported to her husband.

Roosevelt was able to give a nominating speech for Al
Smith at the Democratic convention of 1924. Smith did not
win nomination, but Roosevelt was cheered loudly. He
was back in active politics. He was elected governor of
New York by a slim majority in 1928 and re-elected by a
wide majority in 1930. His measures in New York State
during the Depression were good practice for government
action on a wider scale. He began to campaign for the
presidency, and was nominated by the Democratic party
in 1932 to run against Herbert Hoover. Roosevelt promised

a New Deal. He was elected and took office in March 1933.

A great round of government activity began in 1933 and continued through the years of Depression and war. Eleanor Roosevelt's part in the New Deal went far beyond her task as White House hostess. She traveled and lectured. She wrote books, magazine articles, and a newspaper column, "My Day." The President could travel very little and only with great difficulty, so Eleanor's trips were important to him. When she returned they talked at length about the people and places she had seen. Eleanor Roosevelt also held weekly press conferences. She talked about the part of the New Deal which interested her most: the provisions for public welfare.

Under the Roosevelts, life at the White House was as expansive and hectic as the government itself. The Roosevelts were warm hosts. Their visitors included countless grandchildren and thousands of dinner guests; the King and Queen of England with maids and valets; Foreign Minister Molotov of Russia with his own dark bread and sausages; and Madame Chiang of China with 40 followers who clapped for servants at every turn. A long parade of repairmen, electricians, painters, and maids with dust cloths tramped through the house and tried to get their work done when nobody was around.

Above, Eleanor Roosevelt lunches with American soldiers during a wartime visit to Camp Cable in Queensland, Australia.
Below, she waves to departing troops.

World War II broke out in Europe in 1939, and in December 1941 the United States entered the war. Guns were mounted on the White House roof, a bomb shelter installed in the basement. Winston Churchill, a frequent visitor, had his own map room on the second floor. During the war Eleanor made good-will trips to England, the South Pacific, and the Caribbean. She visited military camps and continued to present reports to the President.

On April 12, 1945, three months after the beginning of his fourth term, Franklin Roosevelt died at Warm Springs, Georgia. The war in Europe was to end in less than a month, and people everywhere mourned his death. Later that year President Truman appointed Eleanor Roosevelt a delegate to the United Nations, where she became chairman of the commission which drafted the Universal Declaration of Human Rights. She left the United Nations in 1952 but returned after the Republican years, when President Kennedy appointed her in 1961.

Eleanor Roosevelt did not forget about politics. When she addressed the Democratic national conventions of 1952 and 1956 the band played "Happy Days Are Here Again" and everyone cheered and shouted. In 1959 she became active in a reform movement within the Democratic party of New York City.

On November 4, 1962, Eleanor Roosevelt died in her New York home at the age of 78.

## Elizabeth Wallace Truman

Elizabeth Virginia Wallace was born in Independence, Missouri, on February 13, 1885. Bess, as she was called, was descended from a long line of Independence aristocracy. Harry Truman was born in La Mar, Missouri, on May 8, 1884. He was the son of a poor mule trader and farmer.

In 1891 Harry's parents moved to Independence. Bess and Harry met at Sunday school and became childhood sweethearts. He was seven and she was six. After graduating from high school together in 1901, they went their separate ways. Truman worked as a bank clerk for a short time, and then worked for 10 years on his uncle's farm. After the death of Bess's father in 1903, she and her mother moved into her grandparents' mansion. Bess was sent to finishing school in Kansas City.

In 1913 Harry returned to Independence, and the two sweethearts took up where they had left off. In spite of Mrs. Wallace's disapproval, they became engaged after a five-year courtship. When World War I broke out, Truman joined the Army and was sent to Europe. After the war, on June 28, 1919, they were married. He was 35 and she was 34.

In 1921 Truman opened a clothing store in Kansas City. The business failed. He was elected county judge, served a two-year term, and was defeated in his try for a second term. In 1924 Bess gave birth to the Trumans' only child, a daughter, Margaret. In 1926 Truman was elected presiding judge of the county court. In 1934, with the aid of political boss Tom Pendergast, he ran for the United States Senate and was elected. The penniless Trumans moved to Washington.

Harry Truman (1884-1972)

After the outbreak of World War II, Truman became chairman of a Senate committee investigating the operation of the defense program. The national publicity he received in this position made it possible for him to run for the Democratic vice-presidential nomination in 1944, and he became President Franklin D. Roosevelt's running mate. When he received the nomination, Harry was surrounded by newsmen. Bess said, "Are we going to have to go through this all the rest of our lives?"

During the 1944 campaign, when Bess overheard two women criticizing her for wearing seersucker, she said, "I wonder if they thought a vice-presidential candidate's wife should be dressed in royal purple."

On April 12, 1945, President Roosevelt died, and Harry Truman was sworn in as President. At the age of 60 Bess Truman became First Lady.

Bess was admired for her courtesy, kindness, and composure. As First Lady she never put on airs. She did her own cooking and shopping. She tried to avoid the limelight, and was criticized for refusing to hold press conferences. She often scolded her husband for the salty language he used on his political enemies. During the 1948 campaign Truman referred to Bess as "the Boss" and to Margaret as "the one who bosses the Boss."

In 1949, after Truman's second inaugural, it was discovered that the White House was about to collapse. While it was being reconstructed, the Trumans lived in the Blair House across the street, where they remained for most of the second term.

Harry Truman was President from 1945 to 1953, and is now generally recognized as one of the greatest Presidents. The Truman presidency saw the dropping of the first atom bomb; the end of World War II; the Marshall Plan; the Truman Doctrine; the formation of NATO; the

Korean War; the firing of Douglas MacArthur, an insubordinate general; and a period of political witch-hunting called McCarthyism, after a Wisconsin Senator, Joe McCarthy.

As the end of Truman's second term approached, Bess urged him not to run again. She had never enjoyed the limelight, and a recent attempt on the President's life had especially frightened her. Truman agreed, and decided not to run in 1952.

After leaving the White House, the Trumans went home to Independence. There, Truman worked on writing his memoirs. He and Bess were frequently visited by Margaret, her husband, Clifton Daniels, and their four sons. Like her father, Margaret had also become an author. She published *Harry S. Truman,* a biography of her famous father.

On the day after Christmas in 1972, Harry Truman died. As he had wished, the family gave him a simple funeral in Independence. He was buried in the courtyard of the Harry S. Truman Library, which had been built in Independence in 1957.

After her husband's death, Bess Truman continued to live at the family house. In February 1975, when she turned 90, she was still content at home, watching television and reading mystery stories in her spare time.

## Mary Geneva Doud Eisenhower (1896-1979)

Mary Geneva Doud was born November 14, 1896, in Boone, Iowa. Her family was prosperous. Her father, John Doud, made enough money in the meat-packing business to retire at 36 and move the family to Denver.

Mary, nicknamed Mamie, was an average student. She didn't like books. She found reading much less interesting than dancing, playing the piano, and playing jacks.

In 1915, while the family was in San Antonio, Texas, for their winter vacation, Mamie met Lieutenant Dwight Eisenhower and thought he was "the spiffiest-looking man ... big, blond, and masterful." They began dating.

Dwight David Eisenhower was a poor boy who had been raised on the wrong side of the tracks in Abilene, Kansas. His father was a mechanic. At the age of 11, Dwight went to work in a creamery. He chose a military career as the only way to get a college education. He passed the competitive examination and went to West Point, where he finished 61st in a class of 164.

Dwight and Mamie became engaged on February 14, 1916, and were married in Denver on July 1. Mamie was 19 and wore pink.

For Mamie the military life was a lonely, dreary struggle. She lived in 27 different homes in 38 years. In 1932 Eisenhower met General Douglas MacArthur, who had a bad reputation for leading federal troops against the veterans' bonus marchers, using tear gas on them, and burning down their shacks. MacArthur asked Eisenhower to restore his public image by writing his speeches and his reports to Congress. Then MacArthur took him to the Philippines as his aide. After several years they had a falling out, and the Eisenhowers returned to the States.

In June 1942, when Eisenhower went to Europe to

Dwight D. Eisenhower
(1890-1969)

direct the allied forces, Mamie was left alone in Washington. Their 20-year old son, John, was away at West Point. After the allied victory, Eisenhower was a hero. He became president of Columbia University. In 1950 he became commander of NATO in Europe. In 1952 the Republican party nominated him for the presidency, and he was elected, defeating Governor Adlai Stevenson of Illinois.

Mamie adapted easily to life in the White House. The years as an officer's wife had given her experience in meeting large groups of people. As First Lady she kept to domestic duties and did not take an interest in politics.

She was a good judge of household matters and strict about having things just right. The average wife and mother identified with Mamie. She liked steak and potatoes, scrabble, mystery stories, and television. She liked flowered hats, colored gloves, fluffy dresses, and pink. She seemed the happy housewife—neat, fashionable, and friendly.

Mamie was hampered by ill health. Because of a rheumatic heart, she needed much rest. Before a dinner or reception she would spend a whole day in bed. Yet she always appeared cheerful in public. She had an inner ear ailment which disturbed her sense of balance. In 1917, after the birth of her first child, she almost died of a lung infection. The child, a boy, died of scarlet fever. In the 1930's she had a stomach ailment which sent her into a coma.

Her husband's health was also a matter of concern. During his first term he suffered a heart attack and had a major intestinal operation. In the following years the White House social schedule was cut drastically.

During Eisenhower's first term as President the Korean War was ended by a cease-fire agreement. In his second term Eisenhower found it necessary to send federal troops to Little Rock, Arkansas, to enforce school integration.

Important advances in modern space science were also made during Eisenhower's second term in office; in 1957 the Russians orbited the first Sputnik satellite and the following year the United States launched Explorer I.

In 1961 the Eisenhowers left the White House to live on their farm near Gettysburg, Pennsylvania. During most of the year before Eisenhower's death in March 1969, Mamie stayed with him at Walter Reed Army Hospital in Washington, D.C. "She's been a real soldier through it all," a hospital official stated.

After her husband's death, Mamie returned to Gettysburg. She was lonely, but she managed to keep busy. Eisenhower had turned to painting for relaxation during his illness. Now Mamie organized a show of his paintings for the public. Her son, John, also helped to keep his father's memory alive. In 1978, he published the letters that his father had written to Mamie during the war.

Mamie enjoyed spending time with John, his wife, and their four children. One of Mamie's grandchildren, David, had married Julie Nixon, the daughter of Eisenhower's vice president, in 1968. David wrote a biography of his grandfather, and Julie wrote one about Mamie.

In 1978 Mamie moved from Gettysburg to the Washington, D.C., apartment building where she had stayed when her husband was in Europe. She continued to read a great deal, and she personally answered almost all of the mail she received.

On November 1, 1979, 80-year-old Mamie died quietly in her sleep following a stroke. She was buried beside Ike in a small chapel on the grounds of the Eisenhower Library in Abilene, Kansas.

## Jacqueline Bouvier Kennedy

Jacqueline Bouvier was born July 28, 1929, in South-ampton, Long Island. Her parents, John and Janet Lee Bouvier, were rich, Republican, and socially prominent. Jackie attended fashionable girls' schools, where she was trained to be a lady. Her favorite activities were reading and horseback riding.

When Jackie was in her teens, her parents were di-vorced, and her mother married Hugh Auchincloss. Jackie spent her summers in Newport, Rhode Island, and her winters at Merrywood Estate in Virginia. In 1948 she was presented to society at debutante parties and was named "deb of the year." She studied for two years at Vassar and a year at the Sorbonne in Paris. After finishing her studies at George Washington University, Jackie got a job as a $42.50-a-week inquiring photographer for the Washington *Times Herald.*

In 1951 Jackie met Massachusetts Representative John F. Kennedy, then 35, at a dinner party. The meeting led to courtship and the courtship led to marriage. The wedding took place on September 12, 1953. The couple bought a house in McLean, Virginia, where he learned to adjust to her arty friends and she to his political friends.

Jacqueline Kennedy

In 1954 Kennedy's war-injured back became trouble-
some, and he had to have two operations on his spine.
While he was recuperating, he wrote his prize-winning
book, *Profiles in Courage*. They bought a home in George-
town, and in 1957 a daughter, Caroline, was born. In 1960
John F. Kennedy received the Democratic nomination for

the presidency and was elected, defeating Vice-President Richard Nixon. That year John F. Kennedy, Jr., was born. Another son, Patrick Bouvier Kennedy, was born August 7, 1963, and died two days later.

At 31 Jackie Kennedy was the third youngest First Lady in history. At the inauguration she said, "I feel as though I have just become a piece of public property." But she kept her identity and her personal independence from being overwhelmed by either the public spotlight or the big Kennedy family. She dared to be herself. Her favorite First Lady was Bess Truman, because Mrs. Truman succeeded in being herself.

Jackie felt that her first duty was always to her husband and children. She fought to shield her children from publicity and its possible ill effects. She set up a special nursery school in the White House for Caroline and her friends. Once she put on a wig and nurse's uniform to take Caroline to an amusement park, and got away with it unrecognized. She refused to attend public luncheons and dinners because she preferred to spend the time with her children. Her husband agreed.

Jackie brought culture into the White House. Artists, writers, and musicians were welcomed. She was praised around the world for her interest in art, literature, and the theatre. On trips abroad her charm and grace made her an excellent ambassador for her country.

John F. Kennedy
(1917-1963)

A project very important to her was the restoration of White House furnishings with emphasis on their historical significance. She promoted the formation of the White House Historical Association to assure that artistic and historical objects would continue to be purchased for the White House. She conducted a televised tour of the White House.

During John F. Kennedy's administration there were crises in Berlin and Cuba; the Peace Corps was formed; the Alliance for Progress was formed to promote economic development and social reform in Latin America; tariff reductions were agreed upon; and the nuclear test ban treaty came into being.

John Fitzgerald Kennedy was shot by an assassin on November 22, 1963, in Dallas, Texas. Jackie's courage and dignity helped light a grief-stricken nation through its darkest days.

The summer after her husband's death, Jackie moved from Washington to New York City. In October 1968, she married Aristotle Onassis, a wealthy Greek shipowner. The couple lived a glamorous life in Europe. They entertained many world leaders and society people on Onassis's multi-million-dollar yacht, *Christina*. Jackie was always being photographed and written about, but she fought hard to keep her privacy.

In 1975, Onassis died. At 46, Jackie was a widow for the second time. The next year she moved from Europe back to New York. There she worked as an editor for several book publishing companies.

Today, she is active on behalf of many civic and cultural causes. Preserving buildings of historical interest is still one of her favorite projects. And, of course, she is still the proud mother of John, Jr., and Caroline, who graduated from Harvard University in 1980. In the face of great personal tragedy, Jackie has continued to lead an active life and to keep her dignity and poise while constantly in the public eye.

Lady Bird Johnson

## Claudia Taylor Johnson

Claudia Alta Taylor was born December 22, 1912, the daughter of a wealthy family of Karnack, Texas. At the age of two she was given the nickname "Lady Bird" by a nurse, who said that she was as pretty as a lady bird. She was raised and educated in Texas and graduated from the University of Texas with degrees in the liberal arts and journalism.

On September 12, 1934, Lady Bird met Lyndon Baines Johnson. Lyndon was born August 7, 1908, near Stonewall, Texas. In 1930 he graduated from Southwest Texas State Teachers College. In 1931 he went to Washington, D.C., as a congressional secretary. When he met Lady Bird he was attending a hearing of the Texas Railroad Commission in Austin. He asked her for a date but she turned him down. After he returned to Washington, he kept sending her letters and telegrams and making long-distance calls. Two months later he proposed and she accepted. They were married November 17, 1934, and honeymooned in Mexico. In 1944 Lynda Bird was born, and three years later Luci Baines was born.

In 1937 Johnson was elected to the United States House of Representatives. In 1941-42 he served in the Navy. He was elected to the United States Senate in 1948 and seven years later he became Senate majority leader. In 1960 he was elected Vice-President of the United States

Lyndon B. Johnson
(1908-1973)

on the Democratic ticket. On November 22, 1963, the assassination of President John F. Kennedy made Lyndon
Johnson President of the United States.

The Johnsons brought Texas hospitality to the White
House, maintaining an atmosphere of warmth and in-
formality. Lady Bird was a charming, poised, and friendly
hostess. The presence of two marriageable daughters in
the White House made good news copy. The public sym-
pathized with Luci's and Lynda's objections to the unro-
mantic presence of secret service agents on their dates.
When Luci married Patrick Nugent in 1966, she was the

first daughter of a President to marry while her father was in office since Eleanor Wilson in 1914.

Lady Bird was keenly interested in politics. In the 1964 campaign she conducted the first whistlestop tour carried out by a First Lady, stumping the South. In 1964 Johnson was elected to a full term, defeating Barry Goldwater, Republican Senator from Arizona. The January inaugural was a noisy celebration, with marching troops, dancing Indians, mountain men, flags, horses, band music, and five inaugural balls scattered throughout the city.

The Lyndon Johnson presidency saw the passage of a new civil rights law; the passage of medicare; and the continuation of the war on poverty. In 1966 Johnson appointed the first Negro to the cabinet, when he made Robert C. Weaver Secretary of Housing and Urban Development. In 1967 he made Thurgood Marshall the first Negro Supreme Court justice. However, the domestic accomplishments of the Johnson administration were overshadowed by the costly and frustrating war in Vietnam.

During her years in the White House Lady Bird's dearest project was the beautification of America. She suffered a setback in 1968, however, when Congress slashed 23 million dollars from a highway aid bill, leaving only two million dollars to rid the nation of billboards.

On March 31, 1968, Lyndon Johnson told a surprised nation that he had decided not to run for re-election. When his term ended, he and Lady Bird went home to the LBJ Ranch in Texas. During Johnson's administration the ranch had served as an informal White House where important guests were entertained. Lady Bird had made the 14-room, 100-year-old mansion into a lovely home. Now she and her husband could settle back and relax there. They enjoyed visits from Lynda and Chuck Robb, who lived in Virginia, Luci and Pat Nugent, who lived in Texas, and their children. Johnson worked on his memoirs and on various non-political projects. Then in 1973, after two heart attacks, he died.

After his death, Lady Bird stayed on the ranch. Today she manages the business her husband left and is involved with the Lyndon B. Johnson Library at the University of Texas, in nearby Austin. She also travels widely—to Iran, Italy, and Africa, among other places—and works on her beautification projects.

Lady Bird has not set aside her beloved politics, either. When her daughter's husband, Chuck Robb, ran successfully for lieutenant-governor of Virginia in 1977 and for governor four years later, Lady Bird's energetic campaign work helped him win.

## Patricia Ryan Nixon

Thelma Catherine Ryan was born March 16, 1912, in Ely, Nevada. Because she was born on St. Patrick's Eve, her father, William Ryan, added the name Patricia. She had two older brothers, Bill and Tom.

When Thelma was one year old, her father gave up mining and settled on a truck farm near Los Angeles.

When she was 13 her mother died, and Thelma became the homemaker. Her father became ill when she was a senior in high school. Two years later he died. From then on she called herself Patricia in memory of her father.

After her father's death, Pat went to New York City and worked as an x-ray technician to raise money for college. Then she returned to the west coast and attended the University of Southern California. After graduating from the university, Pat taught at Whittier Union High School in Whittier, California. In Whittier she met a young lawyer named Richard Nixon. After a three-year courtship they were married on June 21, 1940. Their first home was an apartment over a garage.

Richard Nixon was born January 9, 1913, in Yorba Linda, California. He graduated from Whittier College and Duke Law School. During World War II he served in the Navy. In 1946 he was elected to the United States House of Representatives where he was an active member of the Committee on Un-American Activities. In 1950 he was elected to the Senate.

In 1952 Nixon received the vice-presidential nomination on the Republican ticket with Dwight Eisenhower. During the 1952 campaign he was involved in a dispute over an expense fund. In a nationwide radio and television appearance he discussed his finances and vowed to keep Checkers, the cocker spaniel that had been given to his daughters, Tricia and Julie. The Republicans won the election and the Nixons kept Checkers.

Richard and Pat Nixon with Julie (left) and Tricia. In December 1968 Julie
married David Eisenhower, grandson of Dwight D. Eisenhower.

During his years as Vice-President, Nixon visited
more than 60 countries. As a representative of the United
States he was booed and stoned during a tour of Latin
America. In 1959 he went to Russia and met Premier
Khrushchev. One of their most memorable meetings took
place in the kitchen of a model home exhibit, and Nixon's
"kitchen debate" became a part of his political history.

In 1960 he ran for the presidency against John F.

Kennedy and was defeated. He was also unsuccessful in his attempt to gain the governorship of California in 1962. Nixon then retired to private life and practiced law in New York City. In 1968 he received the Republican nomination for the presidency and won the election, defeating Democrat Hubert Humphrey and George Wallace.

Pat Nixon was active in the 1968 campaign, as she had been in her husband's earlier campaigns. She traveled with him across the country and appeared before many audiences. A reserved person in public, she stayed close to her husband and spoke little on her own.

During his first term as president, Nixon worked toward ending the Vietnam War and toward improving United States relations with Russia and China. In 1972, he and Pat made a historic trip to China. It was the first visit to that country ever made by an American president. Also during Nixon's administration, the United States sent the first astronauts to the moon.

In 1972, Nixon was re-elected in a landslide victory. But he was not to finish his second term. The Watergate scandal hit his administration in 1973. Top Nixon aides were accused of illegal activities and political "dirty tricks." Nixon himself was accused of covering up evidence. Rather than face certain impeachment by Congress, he resigned from the presidency on August 9, 1974.

During the difficult days before and after the resignation, Pat Nixon impressed the nation with her strength and quiet dignity. She remained steadfastly loyal to her husband throughout the ordeal. When it was over, the Nixons sought a quiet life at their estate in San Clemente, California. They received support from Julie and Tricia and their husbands, David Eisenhower and Ed Cox. Pat again impressed people with her courage when she suffered a stroke not long after Nixon's resignation. But in 1976 she was able to make a second trip to China with her husband.

Pat is probably the first president's wife to have a museum dedicated to her. It is in her home town of Cerritos, California, in the house where she grew up. There, visitors can learn the story of how a small-town girl became First Lady of the United States. In addition to this honor, Julie, now a well-known writer and speaker, is writing a book about her mother.

The greatest joy for Pat, however, is her return to the private life she missed when she was First Lady. Although she has always been involved in her husband's career, her personal interests have been more domestic than political. She prefers cooking and interior decorating to giving speeches. She believes that "one spokesman in the family is enough." Now she has time for her family. In 1980 she and Dick moved to New York City, where they lived in an elegant townhouse on Manhattan's East Side. There they were close to Julie and David, who presented the Nixons with their first grandchild, Jenny, in 1978, and Tricia, Ed, and Christopher, their first grandson, who was born in 1979.

## Elizabeth Bloomer Ford

Elizabeth Bloomer was born on April 8, 1918, in
Chicago, Illinois. When she was three, her family moved
to Grand Rapids, Michigan. There her father worked as
a machinery salesman, and her mother was involved in
community work.

At an early age, Betty discovered her talent for dancing. She began taking lessons when she was 8 years old.
By the time she was 14, she was *giving* lessons! After Betty
graduated from high school, she went to the Bennington
School of Dance in Vermont for two years. Then she joined
a New York City dance group directed by the famed Martha
Graham. Betty danced at Carnegie Hall with this group.
She could have had a career in dance but decided she
wasn't ready for it. Besides, her mother wanted her to
come home.

So in 1941 Betty returned to Grand Rapids. There, she
worked as a model and department store fashion director.
She also organized dance groups for minority and handi-
capped children.

After her 1942 marriage to furniture salesman William
Warren ended in divorce, Betty met a handsome young
man named Gerald Ford. Ford had been born in Nebraska
in 1913. But he had moved with his mother and stepfather
to Grand Rapids when he was three. As a student at the

Betty Ford

University of Michigan, he had been a star football player. After graduation he had turned down offers from professional football teams in favor of going to Yale Law School. Later, he had built up a successful law practice in Grand Rapids.

When Gerald met Betty, he was running for U. S. Rep-resentative from Michigan's Fifth District. A few weeks after he and Betty were married on October 15, 1948, he was elected. According to one story, Ford was so busy cam-paigning that he was late for his own wedding!

The couple built a house in Alexandria, Virginia, where they lived for the 25 years that Gerald Ford was in Congress. He was re-elected to the House of Representa-tives 13 times in a row. In 1965, he was chosen House minority leader.

During her husband's years in Congress, Betty spent a great deal of time alone. Ford had to do a lot of traveling —sometimes for 200 days out of the year. Betty raised the Ford's four children—Michael, John, Steven, and Susan—nearly alone. At times the strain became too great, and Betty sought the aid of a psychiatrist. Her situation was made more difficult by ill health. She had arthritis and a pinched nerve in her neck that caused her much pain.

Because Betty wanted to see more of her husband, she discouraged him from seeking higher office. But in 1973, President Nixon's vice-president, Spiro T. Agnew, resigned after being charged with taking bribes while in office. Nixon needed a replacement for Agnew. He chose Ford. The choice was approved by Congress, and Ford was sworn in as vice-president on December 6, 1973. In less than a year, more changes came. Congress began impeachment proceedings against Nixon because of the Watergate scan-dal. On August 9, 1975, Nixon resigned. That same day,

Gerald R. Ford

Gerald Ford became President of the United States. Betty held the Bible when her husband took the oath of office. Without planning for it, the Fords found themselves in the White House.

Betty soon found that she enjoyed life in the White House. She saw more of her husband there than she had when he was House minority leader. And she soon had a large number of her own national programs and projects.

Then, not two months after becoming First Lady, Betty had to have a breast removed because of cancer. Her frankness and good spirits about her surgery gave many other women the courage to deal with similar problems.

Betty was honest about many things. She was a person with whom the average American woman could identify. She was warm and kind, but she wasn't afraid to speak her mind. Betty supported the Equal Rights Amendment for women and spent hours on the phone urging its passage. She favored legalized abortion and day care, and she wanted a woman appointed to the Supreme Court. Betty also worked for cancer research, mental health, and the arts. Her husband did not always agree with her ideas, but he listened.

In 1976, Ford decided to run for President. During that year, Betty campaigned vigorously. She was an excellent campaigner, and most Americans loved her. Some even wore buttons that said "Betty's husband for President."

Ford, however, lost the election to Democrat Jimmy Carter. The Fords moved to California. There they plunged immediately into a new round of activities, making plans for television appearances and books. Unfortunately, Betty continued to have problems with her arthritis and with the medical treatment that followed her cancer operation. With typical frankness, she revealed to the public that she also had problems with drugs and alcohol, which she used to relieve her pain. She sought professional help for those problems, at the same time maintaining her busy schedule. Never a quitter, Betty Ford continues to work for the causes—health, the arts, and women's rights—that she considers so important for the welfare of the American people.

## Rosalynn Smith Carter

Rosalynn Smith was born on August 18, 1927, in Plains, Georgia. Her father, Edgar Smith, was a garage mechanic. When Rosalynn was only 13, he died of leukemia. His last wish was that his children go to college in order to make better lives for themselves. To support her four children after her husband's death, Rosalynn's mother, Ellie, sewed for people and worked in a grocery store. Rosalynn, the oldest child, helped out with the sewing and washed hair in a beauty parlor. She also helped to raise her brothers and sisters.

Always an eager student, Rosalynn took secretarial courses at nearby Georgia Southwestern College for two years. The summer after her first year, she had a date with her friend Ruth's older brother. He was young Jimmy Carter, home for vacation from the United States Naval Academy in Annapolis. Carter was also a Plains native. He had been born in Plains in 1924 and had grown up there. But he and Rosalynn had never met before. Now, they were immediately attracted to one another. Two years later they were married.

Rosalynn loved her new life as a naval officer's wife. Away from her small, limited home town, she felt free and independent. Soon she and Jimmy had three sons — Jack, Chip, and Jeff.

Rosalynn Carter

Then suddenly, things changed. In 1953 Jimmy's father, Earl Carter, died of cancer. Jimmy decided to go back to Plains to run his father's peanut farm. Rosalynn did not want to return to small-town life. But when she got back to Plains, she went right to work. She weighed trucks and kept the books for the business. The first year the peanut crop failed. But the Carters worked hard, and soon they prospered. Rosalynn even took a correspondence course in accounting so she could understand the book-keeping better.

Meanwhile, Jimmy Carter was becoming more and more interested in politics. In 1962, he ran for state senator and won. He was re-elected in 1964. Two years later, Carter decided to run for governor of Georgia. He suffered a disappointing defeat. But his religious faith and the birth the next year of a daughter, Amy, cheered him. Carter was ambitious, and he was a fighter. In 1970 he ran for governor again. This time he won.

During his years as governor, Carter became known as a champion of the poor and of civil rights. He also worked to make state government more efficient. After getting more and more involved in national politics, Carter decided to run for President in 1976.

Nationally, Carter was almost unknown. So he began a vigorous campaign all over the country. Rosalynn was an important part of the campaign team. She had made her first speech during her husband's campaign for governor. She was very shy, and making speeches terrified her. But

Carter taught her to make speeches from brief notes, and little by little she overcame her fear. When her husband ran for President in 1976, Rosalynn campaigned almost as much as he did.

Rosalynn was sometimes called the "Steel Magnolia" because she was a mixture of gentle Southern lady and tough politician. She and Jimmy had always been a team, and he relied on her opinions and advice. Rosalynn had proven that she was a good representative for her husband, even though she sometimes disagreed with him. His victory in the presidential race was a victory for them both.

The Carters brought a "down-home" Southern warmth to the White House. Their campaign had appealed to everyday working people, and their style was appropriately friendly and informal. They led their Inauguration Parade by walking a mile and a half to the White House. (All recent presidents have ridden in bullet-proof cars.) Once settled in Washington, First Lady Rosalynn tried hard to maintain the informal style of living that she knew back home. She still wears ordinary ready-made clothes and fixes her hair herself. And she prefers serving simple foods like roast beef and steak to fancy gourmet dishes.

When the Carters first moved into the White House, they filled it. Their sons—Jack, Chip, and Jeff—and their wives all lived there at first. The two grandmothers—Rosalynn's mother, Ellie, and Jimmy's strong-willed mother, "Miz Lillian"—also stayed there from time to time. Having the whole family in the White House those first days prob-

The Carters with daughter Amy

ably made the move easier for nine-year-old Amy. She had liked life in Plains. But she soon settled in at her new home. She became the first president's child to attend public school since Teddy Roosevelt's sons in the early 1900's.

Once in office, Carter began to work hard toward carrying out the reforms in government that he had promised to make during the campaign. Rosalynn also threw herself into her work with characteristic energy. She had her own sunny office in the East Wing of the White House. Like her favorite First Lady, Eleanor Roosevelt, Rosalynn was active, well-informed, and influential. She chaired a special commission on mental health. She was concerned about the troubles that the elderly have and about the difficult life many Americans face in city slums. She shared her husband's concern for black Americans, and favored the Equal Rights Amendment for women. Rosalynn also did a great deal of traveling as First Lady. In June 1977, she made a goodwill tour to seven countries in Latin America. Before she went, she studied Spanish and made sure she was well informed about the countries she visited.

In 1979 Rosalynn again campaigned actively for her husband who remained in the White House, occupied with trying to resolve the situation of the American hostages in Iran. This time she was an even more poised and well-informed spokesperson for him. The Republican candidate, Ronald Reagan, also proved to be an effective campaigner. Although many had expected a close contest, Carter and independent candidate Representative John Anderson from Illinois were defeated by a Republican landslide announced early on election night.

Following the inauguration, the Carters returned to Plains and busied themselves with establishing a presidential library and writing their memoirs.

Rosalynn Carter never did anything halfway. For her, being the President's wife had meant more than just being a pleasant hostess. She was genuinely interested in social issues, and she used all her influence to work for solutions to the problems of people throughout the United States.

# Nancy Davis Reagan

Anne Francis Robbins, nicknamed "Nancy," was born on July 6, 1923, in Manhattan, New York. Her father, Kenneth Robbins, was a New Jersey car salesman, and her mother, Edith Luckett, was an actress. Her parents separated soon after she was born, and Nancy lived with her mother until she was two years old. Then Edith had to return to the stage to support herself and her small daughter, so Nancy went to live with her aunt and uncle in Bethesda, Maryland.

Although Nancy enjoyed living with her relatives, she missed her mother very much. So when Edith married a prominent Chicago neurosurgeon, Dr. Loyal Davis, in 1929, Nancy was happy to move to Chicago with her mother. She soon grew to love and respect her new father, and Dr. Davis legally adopted Nancy when she was 14.

Nancy's life in Chicago was an exciting one. The Davis' lived in an apartment on Chicago's fashionable Lake Shore Drive. They entertained many famous theater people such as Walter Huston, James Cagney, and Spencer Tracy. Nancy attended the prestigious Girls' Latin School. There she had many friends and was active in student government and dramatics. At 16, she made her debut at the exclusive Casino Club.

After she graduated from high school, Nancy majored in drama at Smith College in Northampton, Massachusetts. Nancy knew she wanted to be an actress like her mother. So helped by her mother's friend, actress Zasu Pitts, she began to perform on the New York stage following graduation. In 1949 Nancy went to Hollywood and signed a contract with Metro-Goldwyn-Mayer.

Between 1949 and 1956, Nancy made 11 movies. She frequently played the role of a young, suburban wife, and reviewers were impressed with her warmth, vibrancy, and charm. Nancy was very popular in Hollywood and dated many leading men, including Clark Gable and Cary Grant.

Nancy Davis met fellow actor Ronald Reagan when he was president of the Screen Actors Guild. Her name had turned up on a mailing list for Communist literature, and her director, Mervyn LeRoy, suggested she explain the mistake to Reagan. Nancy did, and she was as impressed with him as he was with her. A year later, on March 4, 1952, Nancy Davis and Ronald Reagan were married.

In 1957 Nancy made her last film, "Hellcats of the Navy," with her new husband. Ronald played her fiance. After that, Nancy was happy to give up her acting career. She had often told her friends that what she wanted most out of life was to be the wife of the man she loved and the mother of their children. As Mrs. Ronald Reagan and mother of two children, Patricia, born in 1952, and Ronald ("Skipper"), born in 1958, Nancy's wish came true.

Meanwhile, Ronald Reagan was becoming more and more interested in politics. Nancy knew that Ronald had many interests outside of the film industry, but she did not know that one of them would soon change their lives.

Ronald soon began making political speeches. After one rousing speech in 1964, given in support of Presidential candidate Barry Goldwater, he decided to run for governor of California. Nancy supported him 100 percent, and she was overjoyed when he won the 1966 election. Nancy felt strongly about preserving her personal privacy, however, and preferred to be a quiet governor's wife. Although she was always interested in her husband's work, she still found time to pursue her interest in interior decorating and redecorated both their home and Ronald's office.

Nancy Reagan did have one favorite social project that she became involved in when Ronald was governor of California. Because she was interested in health care, Nancy visited many hospitals. One day she visited the Pacific State Hospital, and she saw the Foster Grandparents program in operation. This program brought together elderly people and mentally retarded children. Nancy was excited by the program's good results and told Ronald about it. He saw that the program was expanded to all of California's state hospitals. And gradually it was expanded to include deaf children and juvenile delinquents.

After Reagan's two terms as California's governor were over, supporters urged him to run for President of the United States. But in 1975, Reagan was undecided about running, and he started campaigning too late to defeat the incumbent President, Gerald R. Ford, at the Republican convention that year. But right after the convention, Reagan started to organize for the 1980 election, and he remained active in Republican politics during the four years of the Carter administration.

During the 1980 campaign against President Carter and independent candidate John Anderson, Nancy was again at her husband's side. Everyone knew that Nancy and Ronald were a team. Nancy strongly supported Ronald's views, and she also made sure that he didn't get too tired while campaigning. Nancy's presence at political gatherings visibly boosted Reagan's confidence. When she was nearby, Reagan, who referred to his wife as "Mommy," always gave a better performance.

After vigorous campaigning, Ronald Reagan was declared the 40th President of the United States in a landslide victory. On election evening when he introduced Nancy to his cheering supporters, he said that being the nation's First Lady would not be a new title for Nancy because, "She's been the first lady of my life for a long time."

Ronald Reagan

Ronald Wilson ("Dutch") Reagan was born on February 6, 1911, in Tampico, Illinois. Although his life began in a small Midwestern town, by the time he was 35, he was a successful Hollywood film star. Between the ages of 27 and 54, he made 54 movies.

Reagan became involved in politics during his middle years, but in spite of his wealth and fame by then, he never forgot the small town values of his growing-up years.

In campaigning for the Presidency, he urged Americans to express pride in their country, and he promised that everyone working together could solve the nation's problems. Reagan advocated tax cuts, as he had done in California. He opposed "big government" and claimed that fewer governmental regulations would result in more efficient government. While he knew the Presidency would be a difficult job, Reagan was confident he would be a good leader. And Nancy was committed to helping her husband reach his goals.

When she became First Lady, Nancy Reagan continued her support of Foster Grandparents and drug abuse rehabilitation programs. And she placed the redecorating of the White House family quarters to make a comfortable home for herself and her husband as one of her top priorities. Both of them enjoyed spending quiet evenings home together. (For the first time since the Eisenhower years, there would be no children living at the White House. Patti, an aspiring actress and entertainer, lived in California, and Ronnie was a dancer with the Joffrey Ballet Company in New York City.)

President and Mrs. Reagan with family members on Inauguration Day, including their daughter Patti (seated, second from right), and son, Ronald (standing, right). Reagan's two children from his first marriage to actress Jane Wyman are Maureen (seated, second from left) and Michael (standing, third from left), holding his son Cameron.

Long admired for her poise and sense of style and a veteran of the "Best Dressed" list, Nancy often wears the finest designer fashions. But she was expected to bring not only an aura of elegance and formality to the White House, but a sense of warmth and graciousness as well. "She's a very caring person," said a close friend before the inauguration, "As everyone will discover when she's in the White House."